Introduction

This book is not intended to take away from my fellow man, but help enhance your mates relationship with you to better understand the person they are with or looking for, and for those that are lost help them better understand themselves. We are all different, and that knowledge

Road Map
A Woman's Guide To A Good Man

doesn't require a Ph.D. Every human being is fundamentally different, physically, emotionally, and even in terms of character traits. Even if we use gender as a parameter, we will see that the way we reason and act is very different. Men and women have different ways of thinking, different ways of looking at issues; and different behaviors in social groups. Yet, amongst the same sex, there is still a wide variation of behaviors and personalities if we look at social situations like marriage and relationships.

There are men who are great at being emotionally present in their relationships and yet there are many more others who aren't. This predisposition is a very important part of personality that can be shaped by experience and model figures. A man could be emotionally absent due to a bad experience in a previous relationship where he gave all his heart. It could also be because of temperament and social norms and expectations.

In this book, we will analyze together the many different types of men out there and how best you as a woman can identify the right fit for you. The aim of this book is to help you find a man that will shower you with great love, be appreciative, and deserving of you. In this book, we will walk through some general truths, some facts, and some ideas surrounding men and how you can navigate all these to

Road Map
A Woman's Guide To A Good Man

select the right man for yourself. I want to share this knowledge with you so that your search for love and the right partner will be much easier than if you had to do it on your own without guidance. Before we start I want to believe that you already know that you have to put in efforts to make your relationship work. You have to understand that reading this

Road Map
A Woman's Guide To A Good Man

book without actively using the knowledge in it will not solve any problem for you and will not make you any smarter in identifying the wrong kind of man. You have to be able to put into practice what you will learn in this book. The knowledge you will get in this book will help you understand men the more and how to keep the one you want as

Road Map
A Woman's Guide To A Good Man

you discard the one you don't want. It will help you understand how to be in a long-term relationship with the right man for you in a way that will be will be worth your while in terms of time, love, and even your life. The points in this book are very clear and succinct. They are straight to the point. I will not waste unnecessary time laboring the

Road Map
A Woman's Guide To A Good Man

point when it could be easily understood. I am going to stay away from relationship as it pertains to religion because I believe that most religions preach love and there is no point trying to bring up points that will be subjected to religious debate, besides I want to help you find the right man in a way that my

Road Map
A Woman's Guide To A Good Man

points do not conflict with your personal and religious beliefs.

This book is not about knowing how to change men—this will be a serious mistake. It is about empowering you so that you can identify the right one. If you consider how hard it is to change yourself, you'll understand what little chance you have in trying to change others. This book is about giving you sure tips that will keep you off those men with personalities and character traits that will stifle your happiness and life's growth. If it feels like you are doing all the work to make your relationship grow and survive, then this book is right for you. If you feel your 45 year-old man acts like he's 21, then you are to make this book your companion.

Road Map
A Woman's Guide To A Good Man

If you want love, then you have to keep this book handy, except you are not looking for this. But I think we all want to be loved, whether we are men, women, boys, or girls—even politicians and superheroes. Without love, there is no connection in the way that matter. When we don't feel loved, we feel rejected, lonely, and even angry. We feel

Road Map
A Woman's Guide To A Good Man

vulnerable and lost and this is not even a gender thing. It happens whether you are a man or a woman. When we delve into the analysis of the different types of men, you will discover that some men want love even more than the many women. You will find that not all men have lost their heart. Some are out there looking for a connection that has meaning

Road Map
A Woman's Guide To A Good Man

and when we understand this, it is easier for both men and women to increase their chances of succeeding since they know what they want and they can work together as a team. The task is to help women understand men. Since we all want love, then it means both men and women have the same goals, the same desires and wishes and with my

Road Map
A Woman's Guide To A Good Man

knowledge, I will help you to find this common ground in your relationship.

So whether you are reading this book as a man or as a woman hoping to better understand her partner, seeing how you or your partner is reflected in this book will enable you to make the necessary adjustment to the behaviors and expectation.

Road Map
A Woman's Guide To A Good Man

Read and enjoy!

Chapter 1: The Cheating Man

Chapter 2: The Commitment Man

Chapter 3: The Never Ready Guy

Chapter 4: The Needy Man

Chapter 5: The Solitary Man

Chapter 6: The Egotistic Man

Chapter 7: The Giving Man

Chapter 8: The Floating Man

Road Map
A Woman's Guide To A Good Man

Chapter 9: The Angry Guy

Chapter 10: The Mama's Boy

Chapter 11: The Jealous Guy

Chapter 12: The Paranoid Man

Chapter 13: The Always Right Man

Chapter 14: The OCD Man

Road Map
A Woman's Guide To A Good Man

Infidelity is something almost every woman prays to not encounter and can be something that is difficult to handle. It is even more difficult if the person engaging in it is a very good player but that doesn't matter anyway because I will be highlighting here, signs for you to know whether you are just being jealous or your partner is actually cheating on you, so you can either make the decision to stay or leave the relationship.

First of all, we all know that the world has become increasingly social these days. Phones are always vibrating by the seconds from calls and social media notifications, so it won't be unusual to see you and your partner often taking a lot of calls and messages from people. Sometimes there will be a need for privacy when you want to make or receive these calls, and that's OK. But if your man runs to the other room every time the phone rings, that might be a sign that there is a lot more than the usual ordinary privacy going on. Yes, not many men will want to share everything with you 100%

Road Map
A Woman's Guide To A Good Man

especially if the nature of their job is sensitive, but if this is the case, the retreats will not be frequent. But if it isn't, you might want to consider ease dropping to know for sure. Still talking about phones, most people do not delete their old messages, at least not until they have fully exhausted the storage space. But if your man deletes old messages

Road Map
A Woman's Guide To A Good Man

as well as new ones immediately after finishing a conversation, then there may be a lot more going on below the surface than what you are seeing.

When it comes to cleanliness and sanitation, many men do not really care a lot as you would have probably observed. But watch your partner closely; has he started to make his car a bit

Road Map
A Woman's Guide To A Good Man

cleaner lately? Is he paying more attention to his facial looks these days than he used to? How about working out? Did he all of a sudden start to admire himself in the mirror and spend more time at the gym? Has he started acting happier and more co-operative while leaving the house earlier and more often while coming back later than usual? All these

Road Map
A Woman's Guide To A Good Man

would even be more obvious if your partner up until this moment hasn't been the kind of person that pays so much attention to his appearance. If you've noticed this, then take heed and take more interest in this new activity if you really want to know what the deal is. You might be in for a surprise.

Road Map
A Woman's Guide To A Good Man

What about affection? Is he touching you as much as he used to? Yes, your relationship might suffer affection due to poor communication, unresolved issues, or a recent fight. But coupled with the affection-

Road Map
A Woman's Guide To A Good Man

deficiency, has he started being secretive? Does he all of a sudden have a change in his privacy attitude? Something about you're not supposed to know his whereabouts or who the person he's talking to on the phone is. It will be wise to look into this if this unexplained behavior continues or he is repelling you with odd excuses.

Road Map
A Woman's Guide To A Good Man

A Woman's Guide To A Good Man

The

Commitment

Man

Road Map
A Woman's Guide To A Good Man

*Road Map
A Woman's Guide To A Good Man*

This kind of man is very well different from The Cheating Man in the sense that he values monogamy and mutual support. He not only admires, respects, and values you. He does to that other women too. He is comfortable with women who occupy positions of authority and will even help you get there should you have that ambition.

Road Map
A Woman's Guide To A Good Man

He views you as an equal partner in your relationship and appreciates the role you play. The Commitment Man may treat his partner like a delicate flower that needs to be watched, groomed, and pampered in order to flourish. He may even worship and glorify her by keeping her on a pedestal so that she doesn't fall from grace. The Commitment

Man will help you grow as long as you both understand that you have clear roles to play in your relationship.

But the problems with "The Commitment Man" usually arise when they have a family. The Commitment Man tends to focus on the family as a whole unit hereby causing the attention on you to take the backburner. This behavior can cause problems at the expense of romance.

However, when you are able to discover and remember your partner's individuality and contributions can help restore the attention, mutual support, and relationship that foster romance and yields long-term investment.

The Commitment Man can also be comfortable taking the supporting

Road Map
A Woman's Guide To A Good Man

role in a relationship. For instance, if his partner brings more cash to the table than he does, he neither feels threatened nor does he feel frustrated in his supporting role. In fact, he is very fluid and comfortable with roles and will do his best to be supportive. Also, The Commitment Man due to his loyalty might have to check in

Road Map
A Woman's Guide To A Good Man

from time to time with his partner to see if she is comfortable with her roles, otherwise this might spell trouble.

The Committed Man expects reciprocity. If he gives, he wants to receive even if it's in a different way. He expects to be treated nice, fair, and with thoughtfulness as he has been doing to his partner. He also expects mutual respects and wants expects that everyone knows clearly their roles in the relationship. He prefers predictability, established patterns, and rituals. These traditional roles can really be cool if the partner is not challenging her role in the relationship.

The role assignment structure can work but it is quite fragile. Why?

Road Map
A Woman's Guide To A Good Man

If any component of The Commitment Man is challenged within the family, he may feel threatened and can even retreat into his shell.

Creating a balance is essential and anything else can feel like chaos to him and even make the relationship as delicate as he has been treating his partner.

Road Map
A Woman's Guide To A Good Man

Road Map
A Woman's Guide To A Good Man

Road Map
A Woman's Guide To A Good Man

The Never

Ready Guy

Road Map
A Woman's Guide To A Good Man

He loves the company of his friends and moves around with them a lot of the time. His buddies are usually in their twenties or thirties and gravitate towards each other because of a shared history like high school or college fraternities. Sometimes, he might be friends with people because of mutual interests like gym class or soccer and baseball.

Road Map
A Woman's Guide To A Good Man

This kind of man has a strong bond with his friends and his friends also feel strongly about each other. In fact, they feel that a sudden commitment by one of them to a woman will be a threat to the group because they have convinced themselves that being in a relationship will "tie them down" and they won't be able to enjoy their lives as much as they want to. If they are going to be with a woman in the long-term, she has to agree with their "guy rules."

The Never Ready Guy has a single lifestyle orientation and will encourage his close contacts to be single or only get involved in a sex-only relationship without any emotional attachment and if any of his friends gets involved in any

Road Map
A Woman's Guide To A Good Man

serious relationship, he is sure to feel abandoned.

At some points when he gets the urge for sex, The Never Ready Man hooks up and occasionally dates, whether overtly or covertly. But this guy will almost never date someone that his friends do not approve of, if he does, it will be secretly and he would hide it from his friends as long as possible out of the shame and backlash he's bound to receive if this person doesn't meet the set standard or approval of his friends. The only kind of person he is willing to date openly will be that person that his friends approve of or idolize.

One of the problems that may arise from trying to connect with The Never Ready Guy is that he views an intimate relationship as one that is prone to vulnerability and he doesn't believe that being vulnerable is manly. He sees vulnerability in a relationship as a weakness and when he's hanging out with his friends, he doesn't want them to see that he's vulnerable which means he will probably not take you to outings involving his friends. Therefore,

Road Map
A Woman's Guide To A Good Man

the ability to connect with women is a big issue for him.

As he gets older and becomes more matured, he may eventually find himself and look for a way to open up to for an emotional connection.

But in many instances, this kind of man will probably want to have an emotional relationship because that's what his friends are into and will have a difficult time having real commitment. In some situations, he may actually become a "care-free" bachelor. But many times, as he gets older when too many of his buddies get settled, he might start to get the idea that he really needs a partner.

The Needy

Man

Road Map
A Woman's Guide To A Good Man

Road Map
A Woman's Guide To A Good Man

This kind of man will often be dependent on his partner and will often lose himself without guidance from someone as he goes about his daily life. Often times, this needy personality can come from a history of being over protected of in childhood and even in past relationships. The Needy Man might feel that he is unlovable and therefore

Road Map
A Woman's Guide To A Good Man

gravitates towards someone who shows good interest in him and will depend on them to thrive in a relationship. In addition to this, the needy man might conduct himself in a disorganized fashion. This may not manifest itself in the workplace because there is a structure that keeps this in check. But at home, in his personal life, his difficulty in creating a structure makes him dependent on his partner. Without a partner, he almost will not be able to go through life happy, without any issues. Without a partner close by, The Needy Man feels lost and ineffectual. The intensity to be in a relationship comes at the expense of his ability to learn and understand the value of independence, hereby interfering

Road Map
A Woman's Guide To A Good Man

with the growth of his relationship. The Needy Man's inability to see that he is too dependent on his partner often puts his relationship into problem because he will always be demanding and it will get to a point where his partner will not be able to handle his baggage anymore. The Needy Man will always want to be taken care of.

Road Map
A Woman's Guide To A Good Man

He will always need to be in a relationship. He will always want someone to attend to his emotional needs as well as physical. The demands of a Needy Man can really be overwhelming and could be a lot to ask without the partner feeling resentful and in the end rejecting him.

The Needy Man who always put himself in the position of rejection

Road Map
A Woman's Guide To A Good Man

may actually have done this in many of his relationship without understanding how his role has been affecting his previous relationships. The fact that he is always needy may prevent him from seeing that his action is making his relationships turn sour. Without being able to decrease his demands, his partner will feel miserable. She will desert him or even become unfaithful. This kind of man will greatly benefit from taking some time to look at his needs and introspect about the discomfort of being on his own. As his partner, you can help him getter better by letting him know his weakness and confronting it. Facing his fear is very important and will be empowering for him as it will give

Road Map
A Woman's Guide To A Good Man

him the opportunity to become more comfortable with himself.

The Needy Man because of his nature can become too attached to his family. Don't get it wrong, there is nothing wrong with loving your family, but a man who hasn't learnt to lead an independent life from them financially, emotionally, and physically will spell trouble for you and this can make you not to have a happy family. It is important for you to know where his loyalty lies. You want to know where the both of you are ahead. If you are not careful instead of feeling like his girlfriend and top priority, you may end up playing the role of mother, maid, and lover—and you know what that means.

Road Map
A Woman's Guide To A Good Man

With very good introspection and self-exploration, the needy man can learn how to be more self-sustaining and will see how and why not to depend on you all the time. By so doing, your partner can be better incorporated and you will both be mutually connected.

If you find out that your man is needy, you can help boost his self-esteem by not complaining harshly or criticizing him while making him see the reality of the situation and how it is affecting you. As you are talking to him, help him focus on his strengths and try to make him see the potentials that are inherent in those strengths. It will also go a long way if you can complement him on his strengths so that he

Road Map
A Woman's Guide To A Good Man

can begin to see that there that

he has values that can sustain

him.

Road Map
A Woman's Guide To A Good Man

The Solitary Man

Road Map
A Woman's Guide To A Good Man

This man is very protective of himself. He fears being hurt, vulnerable, exposed, helpless, and shamed. This could result from early attachment to parent or caregivers (or the lack of it). It could happen because of trauma or experiences in previous relationships. Now when you meet these men, they can appear tough on the outside, but inside

Road Map
A Woman's Guide To A Good Man

they may feel very fragile. Many of these men will avoid relationships for as long as they can. The ones that still crave some companionship will go ahead but will be secretive, extremely guarded, and may not totally commit. The solitary man will go to a great length to protect himself from pain and will avoid situations which make them feel

Road Map
A Woman's Guide To A Good Man

rejected. For a man like this, it will be very difficult to get to him emotionally because he is well-guarded against being heart-broken again or for the first time. The Solitary Man may actually love the idea of a relationship but he is not prepared for the challenges ahead. If he gets into a relationship, it will be because he wants to take a leap of faith and see if the experience will be

better, but be rest assured that he

has put measures in place.

Road Map
A Woman's Guide To A Good Man

Measures that will guarantee that he won't be broken, but if you understand him, it is very possible for you to gain his trust, It is still imperative that you understand that he might still leave regardless of this but you will know that it is not for lack of trying. When you are with The Solitary Man, ensure that you communicate your needs and give him the assurance that

Road Map
A Woman's Guide To A Good Man

you can be trusted. But don't blame yourself if he has trust issues. It is not your fault. Just move on. If it doesn't work with him, it could be that he isn't ready and he may actually never be.

Road Map
A Woman's Guide To A Good Man

Road Map
A Woman's Guide To A Good Man

The Egotistic Man

Road Map
A Woman's Guide To A Good Man

You will know the egotistic guy when you meet him. He's always talking about his rich family or how much he spends on what and whatnot. This kind of guy is opinionated and cares a whole lot about how he appears and what other people think of him. If he's in a relationship with you, then it's probably because there is something about you that he

Road Map
A Woman's Guide To A Good Man

wants to show off. This could be your appearance or accomplishments. Being in a relationship with him as you can imagine can be very challenging. In dealing with this kind of man, you have to be stand up for yourself and let him know what you want. Don't try to think you can change this type of man because he's been like this all his

Road Map
A Woman's Guide To A Good Man

life and trying to change him will only be a waste of time and effort. Instead, make sure to sit this man down and let him know how you feel. You could say that, "When we are having conversations, I think there is no balance. I love hearing about you and how things are going with you but I will appreciate it if you can listen more to what's

Road Map
A Woman's Guide To A Good Man

happening in my life. How do you feel?"

Another way you can be with The Egotistical man and grow with him is to urge him to grow up and mature. This won't happen by screaming it at him. Instead, try to shift his focus to the relationship constantly or better still create a checklist of things that you can both do that will build the both of you up. It will even be better if its task that fosters team work, tasks that he cannot merely complete on his own, doing this will make him see that he's not the all-important person that he's been thinking he's been.

You will need to be patient with The Egotistical Man and this is the most difficult part. You will find out that these habits may take a

Road Map
A Woman's Guide To A Good Man

while before they go away. So you just have to be patient.

Occasionally, from time to time, this man might slip back into 'ego mode' despite days or even weeks of improvement. A great way to address this is to bring him back immediately you notice that he's derailing. How can this be done? Agree to an action or phrase that will signal that he's derailing. It could be something you both find funny and this can take the pressure off of pointing it out yourself. You can use a hand gesture to signal "Cut the crap." You can sing a line from Luther Vandross song, "There's Nothing Better Than Love." Or say something like, "Let me get myself a cup of water to prepare myself for this." The idea is not to be sarcastic but to bring your man back when you find that he's derailing. You can pick an inside joke that only the both of you share.

If you want to still be in a relationship with The Egotistical Man, you need to be realistic about the likelihood that he's going to change and start to accept the other parts of him that

Road Map
A Woman's Guide To A Good Man

is selfish and that you may not agree with. It is only then that you can start to have some peace in the relationship.

If on the other hand you feel that the relationship is not making you happy and healthy, get out of it. It is not always healthy to stay with The Egotist Man as he may not want to change in the ways that you need him to. If he doesn't work on the relationship, then you may continue to feel depressed, drained emotionally, and unappreciated. It may even be better for you to just quit the relationship totally and move on to something that's much healthier for you.

Road Map
A Woman's Guide To A Good Man

Road Map
A Woman's Guide To A Good Man

The Giving Man

Road Map
A Woman's Guide To A Good Man

It is often difficult to not get hooked to this kind of man. This is because when you start dating, you receive a lot of compliments and gifts as they are appreciating you. The Giving Man will take you to fancy restaurants and buy you

Road Map
A Woman's Guide To A Good Man

gifts just cause. If he is unable to make it to a big day in your life, be rest assured that h will make up for it with a tiara. The Giving Man is not afraid to spend money to keep you and even when he's not so buoyant, he believes an expensive treat will account for his shortcomings. Usually, he is a hard working person and is likely to own his business or be in top

Road Map
A Woman's Guide To A Good Man

management in a reputable organization. He is always meeting clients and business partners. He is out of town every other weekend and compensates his inability to spend time with you by buying you luxury items that will make your friends jealous. Now, there is nothing wrong with being ambitious and successful. But what becomes a problem is when your identity becomes tied to his job or money. The Giving Man may see you as an item that money can retain and that is a major problem because he might start to feel that the money, comfort, or protection he's offering is what's keeping you around. If this is what you are dealing with, you need to have a deep conversation with this kind

Road Map
A Woman's Guide To A Good Man

of man. Often, he will try to brush your thoughts away by saying that he's being a provider and ensuring that you never have to worry about anything. But it is in you place to make him understand that gifts should not substitute for his care, his conversations, his presence, and his attention. Often times, The Giving Man will easily change but

Road Map
A Woman's Guide To A Good Man

not when he is also narcissist

which means you are going to

have a problem. A narcissistic

giving man will shower you with

gifts and compliments, not

because they think you'll love it

but because they think you will

appreciate them for taking care of

you—and this is not healthy. For

the narcissistic giving man, there

is no room for you to show up

Road Map
A Woman's Guide To A Good Man

because it is all about this person. This person will not be attending to your needs whether emotional or physical. Instead, the conversation will be about them.

Road Map
A Woman's Guide To A Good Man

Road Map
A Woman's Guide To A Good Man

The Floating Man

Road Map
A Woman's Guide To A Good Man

This kind of man doesn't really know what he wants in a relationship. If you are spending so much time with person, you might get up getting disappointed. The floating man finds it difficult to commit as he's not sure of what he wants. He's talking about kids one day and then the next time, he's talking about how much excitement

Road Map
A Woman's Guide To A Good Man

singlehood offer. This kind of man is usually available on the market but don't think he's ready to commit to you or anyone especially if he just got dumped in his previous relationship. For the floating man, he doesn't think anything is wrong with him and will rather blame his ex for his current predicament. He hardly takes responsibility and learns from his mistakes. He is not ready to work or grow himself after his break up so he can be a better man. If you have been hanging out lately with this person, you have to ask him what he wants and what he's looking for. Ask him a few questions to get his feelings on what you consider important to you for example on the issue of marriage and kids. If he's out of

Road Map
A Woman's Guide To A Good Man

alignment or does not feel the same way you do, it's best to stay away from him because you will get no benefit from hanging around him. The floating man doesn't want to improve his life.

He's not motivated to do much and is not very accountable for his actions. He is not accountable to you and won't be to other people or anyone else. He is lazy and will get lazy about you. For most men, their life's aim is something that is critical to their overall well-being. So, if they find it difficult to trust people or do things themselves, they can't show up for you in the way you expect them to.

Road Map
A Woman's Guide To A Good Man

Road Map
A Woman's Guide To A Good Man

The Angry Guy

Road Map
A Woman's Guide To A Good Man

There are lots of guys out there with reactions that are consistently overboard and this should be red flag for you if you happen to be in a relationship with this man. I think as a human being, we all know what an appropriate response is and what an inappropriate response is. We know when someone is just unnecessarily trying to flex muscle

Road Map
A Woman's Guide To A Good Man

and exert unnecessary power and influence. It is normal to get angry but it is just not normal to do it all the time. A man who explodes all the time over the smallest of things can really be a source of danger to you, physically and emotionally. Does he snap when you get home late? Does he bark when someone gets your order wrong at the restaurant? What happens when you miss his call? Does he call to ask why in a concerned way or does he just scream at you for no good reason? A super angry guy is not the kind of guy you should stay with. The kind of man you want to be with is one that is responsive and not reactive. You want to talk to a person who understand their

Road Map
A Woman's Guide To A Good Man

feelings and where it is coming from.

A man who gets angry all the time can treat you with cruelty and rudeness and that could be hard to take for anyone whether man or woman. Your partner may treat you with rudeness or impatience and may be controlling, physical, and critical than necessary. You may often sense an increase in the degree of unhappiness in your spouse that may not be easy to understand. With some angry men, you may experience an increase in happiness as a result of being involved in an affair.

Road Map
A Woman's Guide To A Good Man

Road Map
A Woman's Guide To A Good Man

The Mama's Boy

Road Map
A Woman's Guide To A Good Man

It is not a bad thing to be in love with a man who loves his mom. After all, one day when you have your kids, you wouldn't want them to hate you. But then, no woman wants to be in a relationship with a man who is totally controlled by his mother. If he calls his mom every time he's stuck in a rut or whenever he is in one form of challenge or the

Road Map
A Woman's Guide To A Good Man

other, especially when he's over 25, you need to be on the high alert for the mommy's boy. You need to start raising eyebrows. The mama's boy has very positive sides. He is usually understanding towards women and could be very thoughtful especially if he was raised by a single mom. The time he spends with his, the speech he receives, the lectures

Road Map
A Woman's Guide To A Good Man

he listens to can be very beneficial in the sense that The Mama's Boy tends to be very perceptive, chivalrous, and knows how to appeal to women's emotion. He also tends to be very respectful and kind. He hardly will be type to engage in domestic violence, which is a major plus. He makes a very loving partner

Road Map
A Woman's Guide To A Good Man

But sometimes, the negatives could totally outweigh the positives and could be a deal-breaker in many cases and that's where you have to open your eyes so you don't get your heart-broken. Here are the signs you have to watch out for.

First of all, The Mama's Boy doesn't know about boundaries. And so does his mother. His mom

Road Map
A Woman's Guide To A Good Man

will usually be intrusive; coming over to the house unannounced every week for the flimsiest of reasons such as checking up on him to see that he's feeding well, sleeping well, and resting well. Sometimes, she might even drive over 70 kilometers just to say hi. Then, you start to wonder why a phone was invented?

Road Map
A Woman's Guide To A Good Man

Secondly, The Mama Boy's mama cannot be wrong. She's perfect and that's why he would do everything for her even to your detriment. Of course, the mama is occasionally a needy woman who wants to tell his son all that happened to her every day. So your man spends an hour on the phone catching up with his mum while you rot away on the sofa.

Road Map
A Woman's Guide To A Good Man

Because The Mama's Boy idolizes his mom, your opinion will take second place besides that of his mom. Even if you both agree on a decision, his mom's opinion will end up trumping your joint decision because "she's mom and mom knows better".

Prepare to also do the laundry and all the other annoying chores yourself because mom always does the chores. As you are struggling with the chores, prepare to also struggle for mom's affection. If mom-in-law is always kissing and hugging your man, then you chores are the least of your problems. The Mama's Boy Mama might occasionally throw verbal jabs at you whether directly or indirectly. The way you do things might occasionally upset her. Nothing is ever good for her. Nothing is ever good for her son.

You know what else you should watch out for? If he compares your cooking or the way you do things to how his mom does. This will probably annoy you and even blow your emotions out of the water. When this happens, you must address it immediately.

Road Map
A Woman's Guide To A Good Man

Don't let the sun go down without sitting him down to let him know that you are not his mama and he should start adjusting. Take this very seriously. The place of a lover is different from that of a mother. You are a unique person with different upbringing and perspectives towards things and life in general. Make him understand this because the

Road Map
A Woman's Guide To A Good Man

moment he starts comparing you with his mother, your relationship is on a dangerous descent. He might say something mild like, "mom is the best" or "sorry, you can't beat my mom."

Another sign to watch out for is if they talk every day. Picture this: you come home from work, you are so tired, someone even pissed you off at work and then you

Road Map
A Woman's Guide To A Good Man

need someone to talk to home. But when got to your bedroom, you found that your man is talking to his mom. He spent an hour talking to her yesterday. He spent the last weekend with her, and she's planning to see him next week. When this happens, you need to start asking yourself who is the girlfriend (or wife).

Road Map
A Woman's Guide To A Good Man

So what should you do when you find out that your man is a mommy's boy? The first thing to do is understand that for many grown parents and children, balancing closeness and distance in a relationship is not easy and can make them exaggerate feelings of distance to the point of panic. This may be the case with your lover and his mom.

Road Map
A Woman's Guide To A Good Man

But you should not make the mistake of making your lover feel that he has to choose between you and his mother. In the end, he will most likely choose his mother which will be bad for you. And even if he chooses you, you don't want to be in a relationship where you are hated by your mother-in-law. Instead, make him understand that there is a

Road Map
A Woman's Guide To A Good Man

problem and help him find a way to manage his intrusive parent. It will not be easy in the beginning but it will be worth it in the end.

Talk to your spouse, and be very careful of the way you present the case. Don't present his mom as a threat, if you do, he might want to avoid talking about the subject and shut you off. You don't want to put him on the defensive. If you approach the issue from a critical perspective, he will be more protective of his mom which may make you feel alienated, which you do not want.

Instead, make him understand that you love him but you need more of his attention and support. Ask him if he will like more attention from you. The next time he wants to go see his

Road Map
A Woman's Guide To A Good Man

mom, ask him if there's a need to do that since he can make a phone call or even video call.

The next time she wants to visit, ask him if he's cool with his mother's constant company because you feel that it often prevents you both from spending quality time together. If he feels the same way with you, you will need to both work on a polite way

Road Map
A Woman's Guide To A Good Man

to turn down her frequent requests and constant phone calls.

Understand that your man might not see his mom as a problem and therefore might not see that there is a reason to talk about it. But you will be able to have a solution if you raise the topic with great tenderness and sympathy.

Road Map
A Woman's Guide To A Good Man

It might take some time for you to experience changes. During this time, take some time to build your own self. Spend some time working on your interests and accomplishments; this will make you see less of his mama's boy attitude.

Road Map
A Woman's Guide To A Good Man

The Jealous Guy

Road Map
A Woman's Guide To A Good Man

Every woman wants someone who cares but most don't want a jealous guy. Women want a measure of care, independence, and protection. But when the protection becomes too much that it is feels like imprisonment, there is bound to be problems. In the beginning, the jealousy of a partner might be very endearing and even sexy as it might show

Road Map
A Woman's Guide To A Good Man

you that they care or attached to you. But when it becomes more intense, it can be very scary and lead to bigger problems. A guy who sees every interaction you make as a flirtatious one, who is threatened by your friends or close coworker, who looks for fault where there aren't any may be anxious, insecure or jealous.

Road Map
A Woman's Guide To A Good Man

Spotting the jealous guy is very easy. The jealous guy typically feels that he has a right to know about everything happening to you even more than he is actually supposed to. Sometimes, he will make it abundantly clear that he is watching you. Other times, he might do it in stealth-mode. Don't be surprised to find him checking your phone, logging into your email account, checking your internet history and then justifying his actions by telling you that they have had a cheating partner before or that "if you have nothing to hide, you won't be bothered that they are going through your stuff." When you are constantly being monitored and scrutinized by your partner, the grounds for distrust is being

Road Map
A Woman's Guide To A Good Man

established. The jealous guy is placed by intrusive thoughts. He will create a police-like presence in your relationship. He will try to tell you where you should or shouldn't go. Your privacy will be invaded and you will receive orders on how you should spend your time. He might check your mobile phone to see who is calling you. He might follow you around and even tell which of your friends you should see or not see.

The first thing a jealous guy will do is isolate you from your friends and even family. He may start by telling you how often you talk to your friends on the phone, or say your best friend is a bad influence and don't think you guys should hang out together any longer. He might also try to turn you against

Road Map
A Woman's Guide To A Good Man

people that you rely on for support. Their main aim is to rid you of your support cast and thus boost your support on them so that you won't be able to stand up against them whenever they want to dominate you totally.

So what can you do when you realize that you are in a relationship with the jealous guy?

Road Map
A Woman's Guide To A Good Man

You should first of all take the jealousy issue head on. Keep note of all his accusations over a period of time and it him down to have a conversation with him. Do this when you are both not angry. Let him know his behavior is driving you apart each time. Also, try your best not to be secretive in your dealings. If you lie to him about your whereabouts in order

Road Map
A Woman's Guide To A Good Man

to protect him or prevent jealous confrontation, you will only be reducing the level of trust between the both of you, despite the fact that you have not done anything wrong.

Also, try your best to be more empathetic. Your man may be feeling abandoned and neglected despite all the verbal assurances given. When you empathize more

Road Map
A Woman's Guide To A Good Man

with your partner, you will learn to take accusations less personally and make him pay more attention to how you feel.

It will also help to create new routines and activities that will create more intimacy in your relationship. These routines might help him build more self-esteem. Routines like holding hands in public, nights out together, etc

Road Map
A Woman's Guide To A Good Man

will help confirm that you are not leaving him.

Ensure that you both communicate unequivocally. Use clear language. Be straightforward with what you are doing, where you are going and who you want to be with whether it will make your partner happy or not.

Road Map
A Woman's Guide To A Good Man

Sometimes, there will be situations where all tactics to make him change and be more assured of your fidelity will fail. When this happens, don't blame yourself. Be confident that you have tried your best and he is probably not the best for you. Move on, a better guy is ahead.

Road Map
A Woman's Guide To A Good Man

The Paranoid Man

Road Map
A Woman's Guide To A Good Man

This kind of man has the conviction that people are just out to annoy him deliberately. It doesn't matter whether you are a friend, family or even lover. Easily, he gets into confrontations, behaving aggressively and constantly looking out for signs that you are taking sides with opposition. In a serious case, the paranoia might arise from certain

Road Map
A Woman's Guide To A Good Man

convictions caused by being jealous over little things. For example, going to the kitchen to get a bottle of cold water could be seen as looking for a quiet place to receive a phone call from a secret lover.

The paranoid man is a controller and might often dictate to you who you speak with. He will often ask for constant reassurance that he is the only one you are with. Many times, he could be clingy as well. Often, he will make you earn his trust or other good treatment which ordinarily you should receive by virtue of the fact that you are in a relationship with him. Normally, when you agree to be in a relationship with someone, there should be a certain level of trust between both parties for the relationship to thrive. But with the paranoid, the level of trust needed for him to continue to be with him can be overwhelming. For example, you don't need to always need to go to great lengths and details to explain your whereabouts every moment of the day. The fact that you are free with your partner doesn't also give them the right to check your

Road Map
A Woman's Guide To A Good Man

emails, social media chats, or browser history. If your partner feels that you have to earn their trust rather than it being the default setting, then you have a problem already. In an extreme case, The Paranoid Man can issue threats against you or himself. Now don't think that this threat can only be physical. No, threats don't need to be physical before

Road Map
A Woman's Guide To A Good Man

they become a problem. Threats could take the form of leaving you, taking away your "privileges" or even deciding to harm himself if you don't comply with his demands. The Paranoid Man can be emotionally manipulative and even be violent physically if he doesn't get his request. In this case, you might even be in a bigger problem because you

Road Map
A Woman's Guide To A Good Man

might be stuck in the relationship out of the fear of being harmed physically or that he may do something injurious to himself if you leave. It is also possible that your partner may threaten to chase you out of your home, deny you access to your children if you have or even stop sending financial support to you if you leave them. Whether the threats

Road Map
A Woman's Guide To A Good Man

are genuine or not, issuing threats is a way that The Paranoid Man uses to get his way at the expense of his partner.

Whether or not the threats are genuine, it is just another way for the controlling person to get what they want at the expense of their partner. The Paranoid Man is gifted at using guilt as a tool to get what he wants. He is a very effective controller, using your emotions to work in his own favor. If your partner can manipulate you into feeling very guilty about what's happening to your relationship, then you will be made to want to do all you can so that you will not have to feel guilty. Sometimes this may mean that you have to give up your power and opinion in this

Road Map
A Woman's Guide To A Good Man

relationship, which means that you will be playing right into your partner's hands.

What you can do when you are in the same boat with The Paranoid Man is to first of all set boundaries and limits and ensure that they are stuck to. Don't agree to requests that are motivated by paranoia. Requests must be reasonable and so must his expectations.

Look at why he's behaving the way he is. Look at issues from an analytical perspective. Why is he behaving the way he is? Does the evidence match his actions and decisions? How often do his fears get confirmed? Could he be overestimating risks and underestimating your ability to

Road Map
A Woman's Guide To A Good Man

stay strong? Is he unnecessarily being over-vigilant? Has this approach benefitted him in the past? Will this work for you? If you are being asked to take an action that you do not want to take, ask for an explanation. Don't just accept it. By taking out time to reason with your partner, you will be able to better understand him. And if you discover that his reason isn't genuine, you can take your stand and explain why you are doing so. The more you become independent, the more you will earn his respect. If you depend on your partner too much, you risk being controlled and sucked into his paranoid feelings. Take your own life seriously. Get achievements that will make your proud and you will

Road Map
A Woman's Guide To A Good Man

feel way much better about yourself even if your partner is acting up. In fact, he will even be forced to respect you. Your partner will take you more seriously when they know that you have self-respect and they stand to lose something when they leave you. Your partner will push you over easily if they feel that you are not bringing anything

Road Map
A Woman's Guide To A Good Man

to the table, if they feel that you are dependent on them for support. This is why you need to take care to work on your self-confidence so that you do not get easily manipulated or pushed over. So as you read this, look for ways to communicate and act on your thoughts in a confident and convincing manner. If you think that your ideas and thoughts are right, don't stop in your tracks, but follow through, voice them out and act on them. No one likes to be with a pushover, they are exactly the kind of people who get controlled and trapped in a relationship.

Road Map
A Woman's Guide To A Good Man

Road Map
A Woman's Guide To A Good Man

The Always Right Man

Road Map
A Woman's Guide To A Good Man

Almost every woman dreams to marry a guy who is smart and knows what to do when the occasion calls for it. But The Always Right Man takes this strength too far. He is always determined to win every argument. He many times than you can count always want things to be done in a certain way that he wants because...he is right. He always has a view towards everything and everybody and is often pedantic, domineering, nit-picking, and intolerant of other people's views. This man is determined to win every argument, insists on things being done a certain way, or has intransigent views on everything and everybody. He's pedantic, domineering, nit-picking, and

Road Map
A Woman's Guide To A Good Man

intolerant and can reduce you to a quivering wreck. If he's also a narcissist, then you have an issue on your hands. The Always Right Man wants to be seen and heard all the time. His views matter too much. His reputation is highly important. He craves admiration from you and will therefore do a good job of trampling upon your ideas and thoughts if they ever

Road Map
A Woman's Guide To A Good Man

cross his thoughts. This kind of man has an inappropriate sense of entitlement; he thinks he can get what he wants at your expense.

Often The Always Right Man can court a lot of respect in public but privately, he can be manipulative, criticizing, and humiliating in as much as he gets what he wants.

Road Map
A Woman's Guide To A Good Man

If you are stuck with this kind of guy, you should first of all talk to him and make him understand how you feel. You need to be respected. Your views should not be trample upon because they do not match his. There is no point being in a relationship where your views, thoughts, feelings, and ideas are not being considered and respected by your spouse.

Road Map
A Woman's Guide To A Good Man

Take up the opportunity to tell him about your hopes, fears, and dreams to deepen your conversations. If he is not that empathetic, you need to make sure that he hears you and that it takes two to be in a relationship. Make yourself heard.

Understand that you are dealing with a master of argument. Your views can get lost in rhetoric and logic easily. So if you want to survive, avoid getting into arguments. State your pain and ensure that you are heard. Give no room for argument and make sure you express yourself.

It is normal that after spending a lot of time with someone, you tend to start thinking like them. On deep introspection, you may find that you are caught up in his web of their energy, ambitions, and desires while yours are being relegated to the background. Look inwards and get back your identity.

Road Map
A Woman's Guide To A Good Man

The
OCD Man

Road Map
A Woman's Guide To A Good Man

If you are wondering what OCD means, look no further. It's called Obsessive Compulsive Disorder. No. The OCD guy doesn't have OCD, he just man that acts like he has the disorder. He has repetitive behavior, he is a freak for rules and order, and he can be obsessed about a particular subject or thing to the point that you will both be driven apart.

Road Map
A Woman's Guide To A Good Man

To successfully deal with The OCD Man, you must not always agree to his demand. Don't do things you will normally not do just so he can't feel better. If he wants something in a manner that doesn't please you, let him know. It's his obsession, not your own.

Take steps at eliminating behaviors and habits about him that do not please you or that

Road Map
A Woman's Guide To A Good Man

make you angry and try to amplify those ones you love.

Build fairness into your relationship. Let it even be a core value. If he's obsessed about fashion and you try as much as possible to be fair, it will eliminate unnecessary arguments about spending money on designer wears.

Road Map
A Woman's Guide To A Good Man

If he degenerates into his episodes, express your displeasure in a manner that is clear devoid of anger and aggressive retaliation. If he speaks in a harsh and aggressive manner, let him know that his behavior is unacceptable and is causing you harm. Sometimes, helping someone see that they are behaving in a bad manner

Road Map
A Woman's Guide To A Good Man

pointing it out to them can make them change the way they are acting to become more reasonable and accommodating.

In the end you will realize that some people cannot change or bend. You will realize that there is a threshold above which you cannot tolerate. If you've put all efforts into making the relationship work and it doesn't still work, then you need to get out of it before it becomes a problem that you won't be able to handle and you turn into a victim of something terrible.

Road Map
A Woman's Guide To A Good Man

Road Map
A Woman's Guide To A Good Man

Conclusion

Road Map
A Woman's Guide To A Good Man

In all of these categories of men that we have discussed, you must understand that increased communication, reassurance, and patience are needed to make a relationship work. So it makes a lot of sense to understand the different patterns that men exhibit in relationships so you can understand how best the both of you can relate as a couple. It is best to understand that all these categories are not to put all men into a small box. The personalities of people transcend this as men will draw from multiple categories and may not be represented in these simple ways. Regardless of this, the description outlined here are there to help you understand how men typically behave, what they can mean for your

Road Map
A Woman's Guide To A Good Man

relationship, and how it can help you manage and love your partner better.

If you find that you are the giver in a relationship and your partner is always receiving, then it pays to invest some of your energy into other things so that you can have a balanced life. Ensure that you are giving yourself and what interests you all the attention and care you deserve. Enroll in a class, fashion out the time to enjoy the things you love. Focus on taking care of yourself and your needs. Volunteer for a cause and do something worthwhile. Do not let relationship issues bog you down.

If you are helping your partner is trying to change, understand that there are still potential pitfalls that will arise. As you are helping him adjust, ensure that during this time, you are maintaining an awareness of how you feel. You may experience some ups and downs but it is important that you understand how your day-to-day life is being affected by the relationship. Look out for your emotional health and give yourself enough time to recover. Try your best to not let the

Road Map
A Woman's Guide To A Good Man

relationship consume your life. Spend some time with other people that care about you. Work on a hobby and do some other things that interest you.

As you are trying to enjoy your relationship, ensure that you have a support cast; a system that can be used as a resource. Make use of your support system, if you have one. But if you don't, ensure

to make a new one for yourself.
Your support system should make you feel excited and good about yourself. They should be about people that you trust and are comfortable with. Your support cast can include friends, family, the people in your religious community, and then counselor.

Go ahead and have a good relationship!

Road Map
A Woman's Guide To A Good Man

Road Map
A Woman's Guide To A Good Man

www.ingramcontent.com/pod-product-compliance
Lightning Source LLC
Chambersburg PA
CBHW070615300426
44113CB00010B/1536